The 3 Y's of Faith

6/2018
Orlando, FL

Dear Morgan,

May God continue to bless you & your family as you continue to say yes to Him, yield to Him, & yearn for more!

We love you.

♡, Mari

John 10:10

faithfulMD@gmail.com

The 3 Y's of Faith

Keys to a fruitful walk with God

Amaryllis Sánchez Wohlever, MD

Also by this author:

Walking with Jesus in Healthcare

Dedication

I dedicate this book to every person who planted seeds of Truth in my heart, especially Abuelita Cloti, Karolina, my *Cursillo* reunion group at St. Simon's, and the many influential teachers and faithful nuns who invested in my spiritual formation at Espíritu (in particular, Ileana and Juliana). Without their loving investment, I may still be craving spiritual milk without the solid food required to live a powerful, persevering, and fruitful life for Christ.

Through this simple book I also celebrate Mother Teresa, whose compassion and selflessness draw me to the heart of Jesus, and whose example inspires me to do "small things with great love."

The 3 Y's of Faith is one such small endeavor conceived, pursued, and completed in love. In its simplicity, I have experienced God's gentleness, faithfulness, and sovereignty. For that and so much more, I am deeply grateful.

Acknowledgments

The Holy Spirit inspired this book from beginning to end and is worthy of all my praise. God humbled and touched my heart deeply through the writing and editing journey and through the 3 Y's retreats I have already led. Thank You, Lord, for calling me to write this book and for guiding every step of the process. As always, the outcome is in Your Hands, and I offer this work to You with a grateful heart.

I am thankful to Fr. Jon Davis for inviting me to lead 3 Y's retreats at Canterbury Retreat Center, my favorite writing spot and sanctuary. I also thank Barbara, Fran, and the women of Nashotah House as well as the various ministry and healthcare leaders who have trusted me to speak to their groups and lead their retreats. I am also grateful to Linda Gilden for the uplifting way in which she edited my book.

As always, I could not have completed this project without the loving support and encouragement of my family and the many special people in my life. I am blessed with the best friends in the world and many precious sisters in Christ. I especially thank Pearl, Karolina, Mary, Ann, and Marisol for years of friendship, for their prayers, and for honest feedback as well as helpful manuscript reviews.

At the core of God's blessing is my beautiful family. Thank you, Russell, for helping me persevere and rise above times of doubt and uncertainty. You are the most caring, committed, and compassionate pastor I know. And a huge thank you to my children — the joy of my life — for your smiles, hugs, songs, jokes, and for being living evidence of a loving, creative, and exceedingly good God.

With thanksgiving for the tremendous privilege of writing for God, I pray that my life will bless others with a closer walk with Jesus.

Contents

"In the silence of our hearts, God speaks of His love; with our silence, we allow Jesus to love us."

Mother Teresa

Introduction

Books about faith are plentiful. And that's a good thing. At different times in life, the right book can make all the difference. My family is living proof.

When our oldest son (now a young adult!) was a baby, my husband needed two major surgeries back-to-back. After the second one, I visited him at the hospital and noticed he was pretty discouraged. Nothing I said seemed to impart hope or cheer him up. I felt helpless.

As I left the hospital that night, a used book display across from the gift shop caught my eye. After browsing for a while, I picked up a pocket-sized book by someone named Archibald Rutledge. Though I'd never heard of him, something made me buy it.

Suddenly hopeful, I rode the elevator back up to Russell's hospital room and found him sleeping. So I left the book at his feet with a note that read, *I thought you'd enjoy this. Sleep well, sweetie. I love you.*

When I arrived the next morning, I found a new man. Russ was sitting up, looking optimistic and refreshed while taking in the clear blue skies outside his window. He'd read that little book several times, and his outlook completely changed. *Life's Extras* made all the difference.

The quick read is all about God's mercy and grace, His goodness and love. According to Rutledge, 'life's extras' are those things God did not have to create, but did. Like sunsets. Butterflies. Dew drops and icicles. Ladybugs, fireflies, and dandelions. And the author's favorite, the spectacular rhododendron.

That little book took less than an hour to read, but it continues to bear fruit twenty years later. Amazing how that can happen.

That day reminded me that God can do anything, and that He likes to use the mundane and simple experiences of life to lift our spirits and transform our hearts.

I pray this simple book has the same effect on every reader, for I'm convinced there is nothing we need more than to surrender to the good and loving God who created us.

Such surrender requires faith, and trust, and great courage.

May you be blessed with all three.

PART I

THE FIRST Y

Chapter 1

A Desperate Prayer

Call to me and I will answer you and tell you great and unsearchable things you do not know.
Jeremiah 33:3

I am a family doctor married to a pastor. Between the two of us, we hear many stories of tragedy and loss. We are privileged to walk with people in pain who trust us with their suffering. We also hear hopeful stories of triumph, love, and conquering faith. Our lives are rich and God is near us. We recognize and long for His presence. But it wasn't always this way.

Although I've always been aware of a loving Creator, I haven't always felt close to God. My loneliest years came after my sweet and joyful mom died. I was only twenty. I started medical school grieving, feeling empty and alone, and I didn't come to terms with this tremendous loss until many years later. Only by God's grace did I make it through that time, for I was not actively seeking Him at all. I didn't realize how desperately I needed God. It was as if I forgot how to pray.

Then came a time of trial during my first job after residency. As an Air Force physician, I cared for soldiers who deployed all over the world. In their absence, I also cared for the spouses and children they left behind. Every person I saw had great needs, while many of my emotional and spiritual needs remained unmet as well.

With a small child at home and a sick husband I couldn't cure despite excellent medical training, I felt completely overwhelmed. My new job didn't help, for the hours were long and the work draining. Something had to give.

One night, despairing, I went for a walk that brought little peace. I returned home still sad and burdened. Feeling lost, I sat on our driveway, and then I knelt. And for the first time in years, I prayed with my whole heart.

It was a simple prayer conceived in the depths of my soul, and it led me to the first Y — the Y that I so desperately needed, though I did not know it.

Kneeling under a vast, star-lit sky, I prayed,

Lord, if You are real, please reveal Yourself to me, because I don't know what will be of me if You don't.

That was it — simple and heartfelt.

There were no fireworks. No visible angels. No palpable signs of my prayer being heard. But it was answered. It was definitely answered.

Chapter 2

Embraced by Love

And I pray that you, being rooted and established in love, may have power ... to grasp how wide and long and high and deep is the love of Christ.
Ephesians 3:17-18

My desperate prayer on the driveway changed my life. In the weeks and months that followed, everything began to change. It was as if that prayer opened a door that was previously closed. A door in my heart, in my soul, and perhaps even a door in heaven opened that day, never to be shut again.

Shortly after this prayer, a friend from church invited me to a retreat called *Cursillo* (a short course in Christianity). I hadn't been to a retreat since high school, and since my memories of the experience were positive, I said yes.

Much to my surprise, during that weekend retreat I experienced the incomparable love of Christ. The songs, prayers, and Scriptures filled my soul and seemed to prepare the way for something new. I felt loved by the people who served, taught, and cared for us. Yet, the most unexpected expression of Christ's love came through a stranger who wasn't even there.

A *Cursillo* tradition involves previous *cursillistas* who write notes to those at the retreat for the first time. I read each note thoughtfully, feeling encouraged and inspired while also pondering who these people were. I felt like a child opening Christmas presents. Each note was meaningful, but while reading one of the last ones, something was different.

I felt embraced by Christ.

A man I'll likely never meet wrote me a letter from prison. Inexplicably, he took the time to tell *me* about the love and hope he'd found in Jesus. He wrote with a sense of awe and deep gratitude, clearly excited to share with me a valuable treasure.

As I read his very simple letter, a warm and loving presence communicated something directly to my heart, bypassing the mind,

You are completely loved.

I felt a perfect peace descend upon my heart — a heavenly drink, if you will. This happened while I sat on a sidewalk pulling notes out of a brown paper bag. The experience could not have been more mundane, yet its impact was far from ordinary.

I met Jesus right there.

During the last day of the retreat, a priest encouraged us to start reading the Bible. He was funny, bright, and engaging while displaying a deep spirituality and a palpable awareness of God's love and power. His faith strengthened mine, and he later became a trusted spiritual advisor who helped disciple me. I remain deeply grateful for him.

I went home committed to reading the Bible for the first time, and the perfect opportunity came right away. A weekend of war simulation exercises was coming that I found exceedingly stressful. So I decided to bring the only Bible I owned at the time: a pocket-sized, green New Testament with Psalms and Proverbs.

In a bus that mimicked desert weather with uncanny accuracy, we drove to the barren military base in the middle of nowhere where God opened His Word to me. During breaks, while my colleagues grumbled about the tasteless food and the scorching heat, I sat under a tree and read. I began with the gospels and couldn't stop reading.

On day one, I read Matthew's 28-chapter account of the life of Jesus. The next day, I finished the Gospel according to Mark. And on the third day, I read the Gospel penned by my biblical colleague, Dr. Luke, the physician. His account of Jesus' healing ministry impacted me so much that I wrote a book (*Walking with Jesus in Healthcare*) based on this Gospel. Volume II will be based on Luke's second volume, The Acts of the Apostles.

During our last night in the Alabama heat, I discovered a simple chapel on base where, at two in the morning, I was still reading. And that's when it happened.

Somewhere halfway through Luke, I had a moment of revelation. I can't recall the exact passage that gripped me, but I remember how I felt. Time seemed to stand still. I was immersed in the story, walking with Jesus and the Twelve.

I saw Jesus healing the blind man and the woman who reached out and touched Jesus' cloak. I heard Peter proclaim Jesus his Messiah, and I saw Christ transfigured on the mountain with Moses and Elijah. As I continued to read Luke's account of Christ's healing ministry, quite unexpectedly, I became convinced that every word I was reading was undeniably true.

This was not just a nice story. *It … was … all — TRUE!*

It was a Peter moment. I could almost hear Jesus saying, "Blessed are you, (Amaryllis), for this was not revealed to you by flesh and blood, but by my Father in heaven" (Matthew 16:17).

9

That night, sitting there all alone, I felt like God shared with me a deep mystery: the truth about Jesus, His Son. I felt like jumping up and down and waking everyone to share God's secret. I felt like Paul when the scales fell from his eyes and he understood who Jesus is — God in flesh. The Living Word. The very Bread of Life.

And, as with Paul, Peter, and countless followers of Jesus over centuries, my life has never been the same again.

Chapter 3

The Importance of Yes

Therefore, if anyone is in Christ, he is a new creation. The old has passed away;
behold, the new has come.
2 Corinthians 5:17, ESV

At the retreat that changed my life, I experienced Christ's love through the love of a faith community. In particular, the letter from prison where a stranger shared God's love melted my heart of stone (Ezekiel 36:26). While reading his words, I felt strangely warmed, as if before a crackling fire that reminded me I was home: safe, secure, and loved.

I recall reading the man's handwritten epistle through tears.

Why should he care about me or about my faith? I wondered. *He doesn't even know me. Surely he has more important things to worry about while imprisoned. Doesn't he have a loved one who needs his letter more than this stranger?*

Why me? Why on earth did he choose to write me?

There was no good explanation for this man's thoughtful gesture apart from God's grace. I now recognize his letter as part of God's ongoing response to my prayers. My experience of Christ's loving embrace and the revelation that came while I read the Bible were gifts of God's grace, and fruit of the first Y — *Yes!*

The implicit *yes* that made me call on God from my driveway followed by the choice to attend the retreat led to opportunities to experience God's nearness. One thing led to another, and it all came from that initial *yes*.

I was reaping the rewards of the exhortation in James 4:8 (ESV), "Draw near to God, and he will draw near to you." Our yes to God opens doors — doors of grace.

Without our yes to Jesus, he remains one we ponder and admire, but there is little relationship. And with God, who made us in His image, it is all about relationship. Peter's experience is a perfect example.

When Jesus explained he'd be washing his disciples' feet, Peter resisted this troubling act of selfless love and humility. The proud fisherman defied Jesus, saying, "You shall never wash my feet." And Jesus answered, "Unless I wash you, you have no part with me" (John 13:8).

To experience the fullness of what Christ was about to do in and through him, Peter had to agree to a relationship that would change him. Peter had to trust Jesus and obey him even when it was uncomfortable, confusing, or even seemingly irrational.

Stubborn and self-sufficient Peter had to choose the way of Christ, the path of humility. He had to allow his relationship with Christ to change him. Peter had to yield.

Perhaps he was beginning to crave this prerequisite to true discipleship, for in John 13:9, Peter responded, "Not just my feet but my hands and my head as well!"

Peter said yes! "Yes, Jesus, I trust you. Have your way in me. Do what you need to do."

This rough man of the sea changed course and headed toward unchartered waters — a transforming relationship, a new heart, and a new life.

I can relate to Peter's experience. When I returned home after another life changing weekend, I told my husband I was a Christian. I explained that, after a lifetime of Christianity, something had changed. I let Jesus take over. Like Peter, I let him wash "not just my feet but my hands and my head as well!"

I said yes to Jesus in a final way and he washed me clean. In exchange for my yes, Jesus was pleased to fill me with his love.

Something new had begun. In fact, I was new myself. I was a new creation, and I knew it. I even had a new heart. And I couldn't wait to see what would come next.

PART II

THE SECOND Y

Chapter 4

The Beginning of Relationship

So in Christ Jesus you are all children of God through faith, for all of you who were baptized into Christ have clothed yourselves with Christ.
Galatians 3:26-27

As with marriage, *yes* is final, but it is also a daily necessity. That small word is critical to an ongoing relationship. *Yes* must be spoken once, and every day.

Our final yes to God must be followed by a daily assent to the relationship that began when we asked Jesus to enter our hearts and change our lives.

In this relationship of trust, we let God have His way in us. Aware that our Creator knows us better than we know ourselves, we give God free reign of our lives. To use a medical analogy, we sign the paper and give God informed consent. We say, "Sure! Do with me what You will. You have my permission. I trust You."

So there is a final *yes*, and also a daily, intentional, ongoing, new and fresh *Yes!*

My new life began while serving in the military, where I felt caught between two worlds. I was part of two distinct hierarchies occasionally in conflict: the medical leadership pyramid and the rank structure of the military. At times, it was impossible to reconcile the needs and requirements of one with the demands of the other. Life as a military doctor was tough for this recovering perfectionist.

I was well trained and confident, having led a diverse group of young doctors as chief resident of a busy hospital. As a doctor, I was used to giving orders, not receiving them. My years in the military provided numerous opportunities to hit my head against an inflexible and intimidating wall.

During my second year in that challenging job, I spoke a final yes to Jesus. For the first time in my life, I understood that he died for my sins. Mine! And I knew that he did this out of love.

I joined a prayer group and met weekly with mature Christians who helped me grow in my faith. I learned about the power of community, prayer, and fellowship, and I experienced firsthand the power of God's Word. It was an exciting time.

I began to pray for my workplace and, within weeks, I met the first obvious answer to my prayers. A new chief of medicine joined our team and brought Jesus to work with him. His boldness impressed me. During an uncomfortable meeting where he went to bat for the doctors, he addressed a high-ranking officer and said, respectfully, "Sir, I cannot separate my practice of medicine from my faith in Jesus."

I learned from him that our faith in Jesus impacts everything, and work was no exception. Far above the medical and military hierarchies stood Christ, high and exalted. He was our General. Above all, we followed and worshipped him.

Shortly after that meeting, a small group of doctors began to meet at the clinic for prayer and worship, and a remarkable transformation followed. The changes were palpable and came quickly. I'll never forget the stoic colonel who, before retiring, stopped by my office to share his heart. He thanked me for so openly sharing my faith with him and then, with unusual excitement and tears in his eyes, he disclosed that he'd started praying to God. I was amazed.

My last year in the military was nothing short of a miracle. I now think of that time, challenges and all, as one of the great blessings of my life. I am especially thankful that through the excellent medical team brought forth by unceasing prayer, my husband was healed physically and gave his life to Christ.

As my relationship with Christ deepened, my growing prayer life began to impact everything. Even the way I dressed every morning became a daily discipline that year. As I donned each piece of the battle dress uniform — the belt, shirt, pants, boots, and hat — I prayed Paul's words from Ephesians 6:13-18, deliberately putting on new spiritual armor. Here is Paul's equipping prayer to the church in Ephesus and to 21st century followers of Jesus:

> Therefore put on the full armor of God, so that when the day of evil comes, you may be able to stand your ground.... Stand firm then, with the belt of truth buckled around your waist, with the breastplate of righteousness in place, and with your feet fitted with the readiness that comes from the gospel of peace. In addition to all this, take up the shield of faith, with which you can extinguish all the flaming arrows of the evil one. Take the helmet of salvation and the sword of the Spirit, which is the word of God. And pray in the Spirit on all occasions with all kinds of prayers and requests.

Every morning became an opportunity to say yes to God while putting on new spiritual garments. Clothed in Christ's humility and love and filled with the Spirit's power through prayer, I left the house equipped to face the day, attuned to my new Master.

As my faith continued to mature, a biblical truth became clear. The invisible armor Paul speaks of in Ephesians 6 is unveiled to the world through tangible actions. This God-given spiritual apparel reveals itself through a Christ-like love that acts.

"Therefore, as God's chosen people, holy and dearly loved, clothe yourselves with compassion, kindness, humility, gentleness, and patience.... Forgive as the Lord forgave you" (Colossians 3:12-13).

Over time, I learned to discern Jesus' voice and the Spirit's leading, both guiding me to make choices consistent with the new person I'd become. One choice I'd have to make unfailingly from now on was not easy, but it was critical. God called me to become a person marked by forgiveness. To follow Christ meant I had to forgive, like him.

As God's forgiven child, I needed to learn to forgive from the heart.

While our *yes* marks the beginning of relationship, a soft, humble, forgiving heart is the indispensable fertile soil for spiritual growth and maturity. Our ability to forgive is evidence of Christ's life in us, and the fruit of our surrender to God and His ways. Indeed, wholehearted forgiveness is essential for a healthy, maturing, and fruitful relationship with God and people.

Through several relationships, I would soon experience God's grace flowing through the spiritual gates of mercy and love. These gates were unlocked and flung open with the key of forgiveness.

I was about to learn the importance of the second Y.

Chapter 5

Healed by the Spirit

The thief comes only to steal and kill and destroy; I have come that they may have life, and have it to the full.
John 10:10

Some years ago, after losing my father, another crucial relationship in my life became strained. I lacked the words and ability to express all the emotions that filled me, and I didn't even know what I needed. As I grieved multiple losses, I felt lost.

In the midst of tremendous uncertainty, the Holy Spirit inspired me to paint. I bought an unfinished bookshelf and, with each brushstroke, I poured my soul's grief and confusion unto the wood while sitting quietly in God's presence. As I continued to paint over days, my thoughts gradually hushed, and I became inwardly still.

With no obvious trigger beyond a prayerful gaze upward seeking God's face, deep called to deep (Psalm 42:7-8). The depth of God's mercy reached the depth of my suffering as I called on Him without words. Like a gentle rain, God spoke to my restless heart, and I was healed. In an instant, I knew that God was with me, that He saw my heart and, loving me, delighted in my seeking — and delighted in me!

God stilled my soul, singing over me, and filled me with His peace. On the side of the finished bookshelf, I painted Zephaniah 3:17, which best describes my experience, "The Lord your God is with you, he is mighty to save. He will take great delight in you, he will quiet you with his love, he will rejoice over you with singing."

As I yielded my soul to the Spirit and sat quietly with God, I experienced His loving presence once more. Having previously sensed His embrace, I now heard His song in my heart, and I was healed.

Thus restored, I realized I needed to forgive the one who had hurt me. I surrendered my "right" to hold a grudge. I let God have His way in my heart and soul. I let God win, which also meant I got my soul back, and peace returned.

"Be still and know that I am God," says the psalmist in Psalm 46:10. The psalm doesn't say, "Be still and ponder whether there is a God." It says, "Be still and *know*." In stillness, I experienced God as my loving Healer, as a tender Father, as my real and very present God.

As we walk with God, we learn that a life with Him must be marked by surrender, for that is the way of Christ, the way of the Cross. Although this is not a popular stance, when we surrender to a good and loving God, what we relinquish is nothing compared to what we gain. The apostle Paul said, "I consider that our present sufferings are not worth comparing with the glory that will be revealed in us" (Romans 8:18). I agree with Paul.

Jesus said, "If you love me, you will keep my commandments" (John 14:15). Though it's not always easy to do what Jesus calls us to do, God's way is always the best way for us.

So the second Y of faith is our need to *Yield*. We must yield continually to the One who died for us. As we let Jesus live through us, yielding to the Spirit through which he lives in us, we experience the abundant life he promised — the fruit of relationship.

In every trial and challenge, no matter what we're going through, we must yield to God's Spirit. Our Creator knows us like no one else. When it is difficult to surrender our dreams, desires, and hopes, we can always trust that His plans are better than ours.

Whether we're called to forgive someone who hurt us, to give up a lifelong dream, or to let go of bitterness, anger, and other toxic emotions, yielding to God is the path of blessing.

In fact, yielding to God is the only way to be fully alive. God's way is always the path of life.

"For I know the plans I have for you," declares the Lord, "plans to prosper you and not to harm you, plans to give you hope and a future."
Jeremiah 29:11

Chapter 6

Why Yielding Means Freedom

Now the Lord is the Spirit, and where the Spirit of the Lord is, there is freedom.
2 Corinthians 3:17

Our oldest son was a baby when God changed our lives. He is now a teenager, and he's learning to drive! If you're a parent, I know you can relate with what we're going through. There should be parenting classes to equip us for this task!

Our son has had plenty of lessons on the various road signs and rules. We've trained him to drive defensively, teaching him to anticipate what careless drivers might do. We have also stressed the importance of stopping fully at STOP signs and discussed the meaning of the various arrows and symbols.

I'm convinced that YIELD is the most ignored traffic sign. And it's no wonder. Who likes to give up his rightful spot in line? Who enjoys sitting and waiting on a slow poke when they can easily speed up and get going? To the impatient, yielding is torture.

But the YIELD sign exists for a very good reason. It is meant to keep us safe. It ensures orderly traffic. Surely, yielding saves lives daily.

When we choose to yield to God's Spirit, we say yes to the only Person who knows us fully, loves us unconditionally, and is able to do anything at all for us at anytime. When we resolve to yield to God's Spirit, we show that we trust God. When we yield to God's Spirit, we strengthen our relationship with the One who has our best in mind — always.

But that's not why we must yield. We must yield to God because, when we don't, we are on a road to nowhere. We are driving without road signs. We are lost and don't even know it.

We must yield to God because that's what His Son taught us to do in Gethsemane, on the Cross, and every day thereafter. And as we discovered on Easter day, we must yield to God because it is the path to freedom.

From prison, Paul proclaimed to the young church in Galatia, "It is for freedom that Christ has set us free" (Galatians 5:1). Though his body was chained, his spirit was free. As with the prisoner whose letter warmed my heart years ago, the moment Paul said yes to Jesus, he was set free.

While imprisoned, Paul used his freedom in Christ to communicate with others the exceedingly good news of the new life available to them, too, as they learned to yield their lives to Jesus Christ.

Paul also spoke to the believers in Philippi about his newfound freedom. He said, "But whatever were gains to me I now consider loss for the sake of Christ. What is more, I consider everything a loss because of the surpassing worth of knowing Christ Jesus my Lord, for whose sake I have lost all things. I consider them garbage, that I may gain Christ and be found in him" (Philippians 3:7-9).

I find great comfort in the lives of Christians like Paul who, having yielded their hearts to Jesus, spend their lives setting people free. Their surrendered lives break others' chains.

My favorite prayer of surrender is John Wesley's covenant prayer. It reminds us of our constant need to yield to God and His ways. I invite you to pray it daily.

I am no longer my own, but Thine.
Put me to what Thou wilt, rank me with whom Thou wilt;
put me to doing, put me to suffering.
Let me be employed by Thee or laid aside for Thee,
exalted for Thee or brought low by Thee.
Let me be full, let me be empty.
Let me have all things, let me have nothing.
I freely and heartily yield all things
to Thy pleasure and disposal.
And now, O glorious and blessed God,
Father, Son and Holy Spirit,
Thou art mine, and I am Thine.
So be it.
And the covenant which I have made on earth,
let it be ratified in heaven.
Amen.

PART III

THE THIRD Y

Chapter 7

A Thirst Quenched

My soul thirsts for God, for the living God. When can I go and meet with God?
Psalm 42:2

Since the publication of my first book, *Walking with Jesus in Healthcare*, I've been privileged to speak to groups of healthcare professionals many times. I have introduced the concept of the three Y's of faith during several presentations. Invariably, I get comments on the second Y, which is not surprising. Surrender is difficult, and perhaps our greatest challenge as Christians.

Thankfully, the third Y seems to flow naturally from a heart on fire for God, though we must be intentional to keep that love aflame. The third Y involves *Yearning* for God and His kingdom in every circumstance.

To yearn is to desire something deeply to the exclusion of everything else. It implies a deep hunger and thirst for God and His ways. We crave spending time with God, longing for the joy of His presence, the safety of His wisdom, and the warmth of His grace.

In the Beatitudes, Jesus spoke of this need to yearn for God and His kingdom and the rewards it brings. "Blessed are those who hunger and thirst for righteousness," he said, "for they will be filled" (Matthew 5:6).

What hopeful words! As I hunger and thirst for God's kingdom to reign in my heart, body, and soul, God's Word assures me that I *will* be filled. My prayer *will* come true. His promise, as always, will be fulfilled.

When we thirst for God, the very presence of thirst is a foretaste of a future answered prayer. God promises to satisfy our hunger and quench our thirst when we turn to Him. God's living waters are ever flowing and His manna never runs out, but we must stay thirsty and hungry for His life in us. Aware of our need, we must choose to come to His fountain and sit at His table.

Psalm 23 paints a beautiful picture of the Good Shepherd caring for his flock. The psalmist's gratitude overflows as he recognizes God's table of goodness set before him in the presence of his enemies. "You anoint my head with oil," notes the psalmist in verse 5, aware of a spiritual abundance experienced in the midst of human struggles. The psalm ends with the confident assurance of a future spent walking in God's goodness and peace through the gift of His presence.

Jesus sets a table before us in the midst of our worldly anxieties. As we invite him daily into the dull tasks and thrilling victories of our lives, he feeds our souls there, too. His Word confirms that he will do this.

"Here I am! I stand at the door and knock. If anyone hears my voice and opens the door, I will come in and eat with that person, and they with me" (Revelation 3:20).

As a young girl, I had several recurring dreams I still remember vividly. In one of these dreams, I sat under Grandma's dining room table wide-eyed and enthralled, waiting. I'd heard a knock at the door, and somehow I knew it was Jesus.

With my gaze fixed on the door, I crawled out from under the table, sprinted toward him, flung the door open, and then scooted back to my hiding spot.

It wasn't exactly fear that made me dash away and wait. It was a reverent sense of awe. I couldn't believe Jesus was right there at the door and about to come in.

My last memory of this stirring dream remains etched in my soul almost forty years later:

Jesus walked into our home.

I am reminded of the disciples on the road to Emmaus who invited Jesus to their home and recognized him when he broke bread with them (Luke 24:13-35). After they grasped it was Jesus, he disappeared from their sight, and they asked each other in verse 32, "Were not our hearts burning within us while he talked with us on the road and opened the Scriptures to us?"

As with the disciples, Jesus wants us to invite him in and get to know him. He has treasures to share with us too.

There is something transforming about inviting someone into your home and enjoying a meal together. It is warm and welcoming and involves an element of vulnerability. It speaks of openness and intimacy. It speaks of fellowship.

This is precisely what Jesus offers us — 24 hours a day! A relationship with Jesus Christ is like a lovely, nurturing, and satisfying meal to which you're invited every moment.

"The cheerful heart has a continual feast" (Proverbs 15:15). A life that abides in Jesus, staying close to him mindfully, prayerfully, and with an expectant heart delights in such a continual feast.

Jesus' promise of meeting our deepest needs stands. He is faithful to accomplish everything he says he will do. Yet, God's willingness to provide for us is not always met with wholehearted readiness to receive. We have a different idea of how our needs will or should be met.

Though we hunger for God's love and approval, we often crave and reach for people and things that can never satisfy the soul. We may self-medicate emotional and spiritual pain with unhealthy relationships, overeating, alcohol, drugs, and sex outside of God's boundaries. The result is far from a healthy and fulfilling life.

Yet, those who discover God's sufficiency hunger and thirst for more of Him even as they train themselves to stop craving the temporal. The psalms are full of examples of such deepest needs met in God alone.

"I spread out my hands to you; I thirst for you like a parched land," cries the psalmist to the Lord in Psalm 143:6. And again, "One thing I ask from the Lord, this only do I seek: that I may dwell in the house of the Lord all the days of my life, to gaze on the beauty of the Lord and to seek him in his temple" (Psalm 27:4).

King David's experience of the third Y and its rewards is evident in Psalm 63:1-3, "You, God, are my God, earnestly I seek you; I thirst for you, my whole being longs for you, in a dry and parched land where there is no water. I have seen you in the sanctuary and beheld your power and your glory. Because your love is better than life, my lips will glorify you." The king sought the Lord and, in God's presence, his thirst was quenched, his heart filled, and with his lips he praised God.

When you have tasted God's goodness, you long for more. If you haven't (recently or during this season of life), I pray this book is making you thirsty. And if you're thirsty, rejoice! The river of life is ever flowing. Your thirst is about to be quenched. Living water is coming.

Stay in the right Streams. Trust in God's provision. Open the door of your heart and invite Christ in. Persevere in seeking God's face, and you will see Him.

I remain confident of this: I will see the goodness of the Lord in the land of the living. Wait for the Lord; be strong and take heart and wait for the Lord.
Psalm 27:13-14

Chapter 8

Yearning for More

My soul yearns, even faints, for the courts of the Lord; my heart and my flesh cry out
for the living God.
Psalm 84:2

St. John of the Cross is well known for his poem and treatise, "The Dark Night of the Soul." As he illustrates so well, our journey toward greater intimacy with God is neither a straight line nor a road paved with thornless roses.

Quite the contrary, the spiritual life is full of joys and wonder, pain and sorrow. Suffering and times when we feel estranged from God are expected parts of this journey that should not alarm or surprise us (1 Peter 4:12). As we follow the Prince of Peace, we also become acquainted with the Man of Sorrows. Jesus is both. Yet, suffering brings its own gifts and rewards.

As I think back to my husband's surgeries and the months that followed, I am grateful for the timing of my spiritual awakening. As I look back, I recognize that season of life as a time of tremendous spiritual growth. It is no coincidence that I came to know Jesus more deeply in the midst of uncertainty and suffering.

During times of darkness, doubt, and despair, it is critical to persevere, and our spiritual disciplines help sustain us. During the dry times we all experience, it helps to continue to worship in community, read the Bible, pray when we don't feel like it, ask others to pray for us, spend time in silence and in nature, meditate on God's promises, and receive the sacraments. When our world seems chaotic, these practices help us become inwardly still. In that stillness, we can know God in a personal way and experience His peace.

As always, the Holy Spirit is our Helper in this process. As when I was led to paint while grieving, the Spirit of God will guide us to what we need, but it helps to pay attention. A deer that becomes delusional from dehydration may not discern a stream in the distance. Likewise, when we fret and let ourselves become distracted and frazzled, it becomes harder to perceive God's presence and follow the Spirit's leading.

A few years ago I joined my son on a field trip to Florida's capital. The living exhibits of native wildlife at Tallahassee's museum included up close encounters with red wolves, white squirrels, and (of course!) alligators. Near the end of our expedition, a moving sight halted my failed attempts to catch up with the tour group. A herd of white-tailed deer seemed as surprised to see me, as I was to spot them. One of them in particular caught my eye while drinking deeply from the waters that served as an almost perfect mirror for the surrounding live oaks.

Clearly thirstier than the others, this deer shut its eyes with pure delight as he first licked the surface and, not fully satisfied, immersed its whole face into the water, appearing to savor every gulp.

Without a thought yet stirred in spirit, these words from Psalm 42:1-2 flooded my soul, "As the deer pants for streams of water, so my soul pants for you, O God. My soul thirsts for God, for the living God. When can I go and meet with God?"

Answering the psalmist, it occurred to me I'd just met God right there. While the animal continued to drink deeply, another passage stirred my soul, moving me to worship our Creator right there on the boardwalk. I heard the breathtaking invitation from Isaiah 55:1-2,

> Come, all you who are thirsty, come to the waters; and you who have no money, come, buy and eat! Come, buy wine and milk without money and without cost. Why spend money on what is not bread, and your labor on what does not satisfy? Listen, listen to me, and eat what is good, and you will delight in the richest of fare.

As these words formed in my soul, it was as if I joined the thirsty deer. I drank in God's goodness, praising Him for the beauty of His creation, for His presence all around us, and for His everlasting love. And I sensed His joy in my slowing down enough to hear His, "Yes! You found Me. Now, stay, and keep on drinking! Learn from that deer to get filled with what truly satisfies."

Having been invited to such waters, why would we choose to lick only the surface or, worse, to drink from streams that will not last and will never satisfy?

During times of spiritual darkness or dryness, we must continue to drink from the right streams and persevere. And when we taste God's living waters once more … *ahhh!* We never want to leave His streams. We yearn for more of Him, and even more! This desire for God and for His goodness and love grows even more as we share this Holy Stream with others.

God wants us to hunger for Him. He loves to set a table before us and dine with you and me. He rewards our seeking with His very Presence. Is there anything better?

Taste and see that the Lord is good; blessed is the one who takes refuge in him.
Psalm 34:8

35

Chapter 9

God is Faithful

This is what the Sovereign Lord, the Holy One of Israel, says: "In repentance and rest is your salvation, in quietness and trust is your strength."
Isaiah 30:15

My dark night of the soul came at the most unexpected place during a restful and abundant time of life. While my husband was in seminary, I gave birth to our beautiful daughter. After years of hectic work schedules and the delayed gratification that characterizes physicians, I traded the exam room for the playroom and stayed home for a season.

My life routines completely changed. Diapers and baby books replaced my stethoscope and electronic medical records. Trips to the playground replaced committee meetings. It was a rich season of life and a much-needed sabbatical where I had more time than ever to simply *be* rather than *do, do, do*. The gift of time brought the gift of reflection and the stillness that can be so elusive in a hectic life.

For the first time since my mother's death years before, I had extended periods of time to reflect and feel, to hold, nurse, and love my daughter and … miss my mom. Quite unexpectedly, it was time to grieve the supreme loss of my life. And what a gift it was!

Precisely like opening a wrapped gift box, grieving involved noticing the emptiness inside the box as well as the brightness and playfulness of the wrapping paper and bow. I discovered a surprising gift inside the box of unexpressed grief — new life!

I had no idea what joy would be released by allowing myself to feel the depth of pain and loss I'd not let myself experience before. Once healed, my soul could now embrace the ongoing blessings that derive from having had such a loving mother. I also stopped trying to fill the emptiness left by her departure, for I trusted God with the grieving process, and He tenderly filled all emptiness with love and life.

God is so wise and faithful. Surely, we can trust Him. And the three Y's of faith help us in that journey of trust and surrender.

Saying yes to God has been the best decision of my life, the first time and every day thereafter. Our yes opens a door to grace.

Yielding to God is easier than it used to be, for God's Spirit strengthens my resolve to yield to Him more each day. The more I know and trust God, the easier it is to obey and follow Him. Yielding, though seemingly passive, speaks a decisive yes.

Yearning for God, I am convinced, is a fruit of the Spirit that lives in us. It is a gift of grace. Like a magnet attracts and draws metal, God's love, once tasted, is irresistible. This *yearning* helps us *yield* and continue to say *yes*. And speaking a daily *yes* strengthens our resolve to *yield*, which makes us *yearn* for more of God.

The three Y's complete a circle of faithfulness and blessing, which is fitting for a God who is Three in One — Father, Son, and Holy Spirit. And this One God living in us through Jesus' sacrifice, by the Spirit, is forever faithful to us even when we fail.

God loves us. He is faithful. No one else speaks only Truth. Nowhere else can life and lasting peace be found.

When we find Him, the One true God, our search is over.

He is our Rest.

So why not take the plunge into God's blessed life? Let go of any apprehension or fear. His love is worth it.

Why not trust Him now?

"Come to me, all you who are weary and burdened, and I will give you rest."
Matthew 11:28

PART IV

Y NOT?

Chapter 10

Free to Love

You, my brothers and sisters, were called to be free. But do not use your freedom to indulge the flesh; rather, serve one another humbly in love.
Galatians 5:13

So why not live into the three Y's? What prevents us from entrusting our lives to God and pursuing His will each day? What keeps us from receiving the freedom Christ died to give us?

Why not live lives that say yes to God, yield to God's Spirit, and yearn for more of Him?

Because we're stubborn human beings, that's why! Like Peter, we're sure we have all the answers, and we think we have all we need. We're inclined to be proud, stubborn, and self-sufficient. These attitudes are obstacles, roadblocks in the life of grace.

The good news is that we can learn to identify these roadblocks for what they are and begin to gain mastery over them. The first step is to recognize them as unfriendly enemies of the soul.

God's way requires the exact opposite heart and mindset. Whereas human nature is proud, stubborn, and self-sufficient, the heart after God's kingdom is humble, yielding, and God-sufficient.

Can we possibly attain this? Countless followers of Jesus convince us the answer is yes. And, as with them, Jesus is our example and our Way.

Christo, the humble king

When pride comes, then comes disgrace, but with humility comes wisdom.
Proverbs 11:2

Jesus personified humility. An ever-present readiness to obey the Father and yield to the Spirit characterized his life. His humility was rooted in an intimate relationship with his Father. Jesus was able to wash his disciples' filthy feet because he knew who he was (the Father's Son), where he came from (his Father's kingdom), and where he was headed (back to his Father's love). I can only imagine the impact Christ's humble act had on his disciples as they began to discern he was their awaited Messiah.

Humility is powerful. It reveals a quiet confidence and a grounding strength. It dispels lies, quiets fears, and walks right past the false self with its proud self-assurance.

Pride, ironically, though loud and pretentious, stems from insecurity. It's a rising tower about to crumble. Pride stands on quicksand, and humility, in its unassuming smallness, trumps it.

Perhaps Paul's letter to the church in Philippi best depicts the extraordinary humility of Jesus. In Philippians 2:5-8 he wrote, "In your relationships with one another, have the same mindset as Christ Jesus: Who, being in very nature God, did not consider equality with God something to be used to his own advantage; rather, he made himself nothing by taking the very nature of a servant, being made in human likeness. And being found in appearance as a man, he humbled himself by becoming obedient to death — even death on a cross!"

Jesus' humility was intimately tied to service and obedience. His selfless attitude came from an understanding of his identity as the Son of God. His confident stance came not from appreciating his own strength and greatness but from embracing his utter dependence on the Father.

42

Remarkably, God's Word insists that, in our relationships with people, we can have the same attitude as Jesus, the unequaled humility of the sinless crucified. But how do we even begin to have Christ's humility?

As with Christ's disciples and committed followers down the ages, we must first recognize and then yield our pride, every day, in every circumstance without exception.

Pride cheats us of God's best. When we choose pride, we indulge the flesh at the great cost of the spirit (Galatians 5:17). Whereas pride actively opposes the work of the Spirit in us, a humble heart is open to God's Spirit. An attitude of humility grows in us as we apprehend the truth of who we are in Christ — God's very sons and daughters.

Humility is the yielding attitude of a heart that knows it's accepted and loved. Like our yes to God, humility opens a door wide to grace.

Christ, the yielded king

> *"My Father ... may your will be done."*
> Matthew 26:42

After being filled with the Holy Spirit in baptism, Jesus did not go on to live a challenge-free life. He was "led by the Spirit into the wilderness, where for forty days he was tempted by the devil" (Luke 4:1-2). The Spirit wasted no time, and provided the opportunity for Jesus to choose whether to indulge the flesh or yield to the Spirit.

So how did Jesus respond?

Famished, alone, and under attack, Jesus prioritized only one thing: his relationship with his Father. He yielded nothing to the devil and fixed his mind, his heart, and his whole being on the will of his Abba, the One he knew would keep him safe.

Jesus disregarded everything except his absolute need for unbroken communion with his Father through the very Spirit that led him into the wilderness. It was this posture of yielding to the Spirit alone that brought the victory.

After defeating the father of lies by obeying his Father in heaven, Jesus returned to Jerusalem "in the power of the Spirit" (Luke 4:14). Indeed, he lived his entire life in that incomparable power.

Before the crucifixion, Jesus prayed, "My Father, if it is not possible for this cup to be taken away unless I drink it, may your will be done" (Matthew 26:42). Yielding to God's will when it meant unimaginable pain and suffering must have been an agonizing choice. We get a glimpse of his struggle in Gethsemane. We also see Christ's triumph in every life transformed through his resurrection.

The bridge between the agony of Gethsemane and the joy of the resurrection was surrender. "For the joy set before him he endured the cross, scorning its shame, and sat down at the right hand of the throne of God" (Hebrews 12:2). This passage helps us understand what was behind Jesus' surrender (an awareness of the joy to come) and where his yielding led him (to the safety and love of his Father's throne).

For the joy set before him, Jesus knelt down at a YIELD sign before his Father and let all of humanity cut in front of him, yelling, "Crucify him!" Aware of a greater reality, Jesus chose the Cross, that we may live and do so abundantly.

Jesus yielded because he knew his sacrifice would fulfill God's plan. This posture was not a sign of fear or weakness but of purpose and strength. His choice to YIELD made way for an irrefutable road sign held high in the face of evil: S T O P. No more. Christ's surrender crowned him with victory over the enemy of our souls.

As Jesus lay down his will and his life, he conquered evil and death. Because of Christ's resurrection, we anticipate a future with no suffering, no tears, and no death. His resurrection brought creation back to life.

Yes, we live in the midst of two realities: evil still exists, and Christ's reign is here. Between Christ's "It is finished" and the final "Amen" of Christ's redeemed, we advance from glory to glory, manifesting in our physical world what Christ already completed in the spiritual realm. As we await the full outcome of our redemption, we know what is coming is better than anything we could ever ask or imagine.

The love of the Father, the strength of the Spirit, and the power of prayer enabled Jesus to yield to God's will. Trusting his Father wholeheartedly, Jesus obeyed and opened the way for humanity to experience the same fellowship he enjoys with his Abba.

Amazing as it sounds, we can have what Jesus had because he said yes to the Father, surrendered fully to His will, and lived in perfect communion with Him. Jesus personified the 3 Y's of faith.

Jesus yielded completely to his Father and let the Spirit lead him at all times. It wasn't the Happy Spirit that filled him; it was the Holy Spirit. Through the Spirit, Jesus led a holy life of surrender. We can too.

Christ, the dependent king

"I and the Father are one."
John 10:30

In Philippians 4:13 (ESV), Paul declared, "I can do all things through him who strengthens me." Once yielded to Jesus and to the Spirit's power, Paul experienced that anything is possible with God, even profound transformation within us.

God knows and meets our needs. God is sufficient. We see this in the lives of the disciples. We especially see it in Jesus, who faced and defeated every obstacle we encounter as we move toward greater intimacy with God. Jesus accomplished this by relying on the same Spirit of holiness that fills us, the same Spirit by which God the Father brought Jesus back from the grave.

The Spirit, the Giver of life, has resurrection power. He breathes life into our bodies, our world, and our relationships. The Spirit brings life.

As with Jesus, God is more than sufficient for us in all things, at all times, forever. As we walk with Jesus, he teaches us to trust and obey our Father. We mature in Christ and grow in humility. We learn to yield to the Spirit and gain a power that heals, restores, and resurrects. And we begin to experience that, with God, we have everything we need.

With God in our lives, we lack nothing of value. Nothing.

So why not trust God with our lives like Jesus did? Why not let go of what holds us back from our own 3 Y's? What do we have to lose?

When we say yes to Jesus, yield to the Spirit, and yearn for more of God each day, life is not suddenly problem-free. The Spirit may very well hurl us into the wilderness, as with Jesus after the Spirit filled him at baptism. But in every trial and in every season of pruning, God's goodness and love prevail as we seek His face and rely on Him.

Paul learned this well. The zealous persecutor of Christians became a new man after receiving Christ's love. His previous life had been marked by hatred. He even stood by approvingly while Stephen was stoned for proclaiming his faith (Acts 7:54-8:3). But Paul changed drastically after meeting Jesus.

Having abandoned his old life, the apostle Paul proclaimed, "But the fruit of the Spirit is love, joy, peace, patience, kindness, goodness, faithfulness, gentleness, self-control; against such things there is no law" (Galatians 5:22-23, ESV).

As we trust and rely on God more, we find that, in every circumstance, our lives can be full of joy, peace, and all the sustaining fruit of God's Spirit. It takes time, perseverance, and patience to arrive at the harvest and taste the fruit. Yet, having tasted it, we long to return and linger in God's presence where we experience Christ's very life manifested in us.

In Jeremiah 30:21, the Lord asks, "Who is he who will devote himself to be close to me?" The abundant life we crave begins when we answer, "Yes, Lord. I want to devote my life to being close to You." And the Spirit rushes in, ready to help us do it.

Every ounce of effort invested in this relationship is more than worth it, for it leads to a life of freedom that is, increasingly, marked by love.

May it be so for you and me, to the honor and glory of Jesus' name.

May the grace of the Lord Jesus Christ, and the love of God, and the fellowship of the Holy Spirit be with you all.
2 Corinthians 13:14

Epilogue

While on vacation in New Smyrna Beach, I saw the most breathtaking sunrise I've ever seen. I woke up at dawn and the waves called my name. Within minutes, my feet felt the cool sand I shared with three seagulls, a few crabs, and an amateur photographer.

As predicted, at precisely 6:33 AM, the sun popped through the horizon like a ball of fire and began to fill the sky. In no time, the darkness fled and all was aglow in stunning auburn and crimson. It was a spectacular display of God's beauty, power, and faithfulness.

Beholding the radiance above me, I recalled Malachi 4:2, where the Lord proclaims, "But for you who revere my name, the sun of righteousness will rise with healing in its rays."

Yes! I thought. *What a fitting Scripture!* The Son of righteousness is our Healer. The Light of the World pierces through the darkness of our hearts and souls and fills all emptiness with His presence and life.

Our desperate prayers to the One who loves us rise on the horizon of our fears like a hopeful sunrise at dawn. There they meet: darkness and light, our fears and Christ's radiance, and the darkness flees. The Son of righteousness wins. Love never fails (1 Corinthians 13:8).

In times of darkness, trust God with your desperate prayers. Remind your soul to wait for its sunrise. Christ will soon fill your sky, for the sun of righteousness still loves to rise with healing in its rays.

"I am the light of the world. Whoever follows me will never walk in darkness, but will have the light of life."
John 8:12

Author's Note

Although I have experienced God in various ways, my greatest discovery about God, to date, is this: He is the Great Paradox. God is incomprehensible, but He *can* be known. He is utterly "other" yet as near as our very breath. He is infinite and warmly personal. He is present throughout creation with great power and He is here, tenderly reminding me of His love.

To me, the paradox of God's infinite otherness and surprising nearness is no longer a perplexing mystery to solve but an exciting reality to embrace, as well as a source of tremendous joy.

I agree with author Brennan Manning that God "cannot be comprehended by a finite mind" (*Lion and Lamb*, p.14). Yet, we must not let our inability to fully comprehend God keep us from seeking Him and striving to apprehend Truth and embrace our place in creation. The goal of the spiritual journey is communion with God rather than perfect understanding (though we move in that direction as we come near to God).

As we experience God, we learn about His character and sovereignty, and we learn a great deal about ourselves. We see our brokenness, understand our needs, and recognize that we are God's cherished creation. We grasp that we belong to Him.

The mystery of God — Father, Son, and Holy Spirit — is a glorious reality to which we've been given a window. We've been blessed with divine secrets. Indeed, "even angels long to look into these things" (1 Peter 1:12). This window into Heaven was flung open through Christ's life, death, and resurrection. Through our relationship with Jesus, we discover that God can be known and experienced. And we learn that we are loved in an incomprehensible way.

Beyond all wisdom, this awareness of being deeply loved meets our most basic human need. There is no greater discovery than the unending, immeasurable, and inexplicable love of Christ. All we can do is receive it with open arms and live grateful lives marked by that same love. And then, and this is truly beyond comprehension, we get to share this love and its Source with others — that our joy may be complete.

I feel like John, Christ's beloved disciple. Drawing you to the love of our Father, the living waters of the Holy Spirit, and the incomparable riches of Christ by writing of Christ's love makes my joy complete.

May you partake, be filled, and live.

The life appeared; we have seen it and testify to it, and we proclaim to you the eternal life, which was with the Father and has appeared to us. We proclaim to you what we have seen and heard, so that you also may have fellowship with us. And our fellowship is with the Father and with his Son, Jesus Christ. We write this to make our joy complete.
1 John 1:2-4

Questions and Scriptures for Reflection

This section provides an excellent opportunity for reflection and spiritual growth. You may answer the questions after reading each chapter, each section, or after reading through the entire book. *The 3 Y's of Faith* is short on purpose, since I hope you will spend more time praying and sitting with God than reading. The book is meant to help you ponder your life, not mine. I am a fellow traveler on the spiritual journey, and these are questions I still ask myself. Our goal is God and His kingdom.

I encourage you to meditate on the Scriptures included in each chapter. They are rich and full of meaning, and will help you go deeper on your own. Take time to reflect on their relevance in your life and use them as starting points in prayer. Consider journaling about what you hear God whisper to your heart. As with the disciples on the road to Emmaus (and as with me at the remote little chapel in Alabama), Christ will meet you there as you ponder God's Word.

The questions can be answered privately or discussed in a small group. They can also be used during a period of time set aside for spiritual direction with a trusted pastor or priest. Be honest as you answer each question. This is about your relationship with God, and we are all on a journey to greater wholeness and depth on our walk with Him. None of us has arrived, but it's exciting to know we're on our way to something wonderful. Own your faith and watch it grow as you nurture it daily.

Search me, God, and know my heart; test me and know my anxious thoughts. See if there is any offensive way in me, and lead me in the way everlasting.
Psalm 139:23-24

Chapter 1 – A Desperate Prayer

1. Recall a desperate or difficult time in your life.
    a. How was God involved in the solution or outcome? How was God's presence evident along the way?
    b. Did you need help from others? Did you seek help? If you didn't, why not?
    c. Did you think to pray along the way? Do you recall specific answers to your prayers?
    d. How would you approach a similar situation now? Celebrate any growth that is evident as you recall that season of life.
2. Have you experienced what it means to pray with your whole heart, mind, soul, and strength? How often? When was the last time?
3. Has your prayer life changed over time? How is it changing now?
4. Do you ever pray *with* the Scriptures, speaking God's Word back to Him and proclaiming His promises over your life? If not, try it! Praying God's Word is a powerful spiritual weapon that will also strengthen your shield of faith (Ephesians 6).
5. How does silence enhance your prayer life? Can you incorporate five minutes of silence into your daily prayer time? Ten? Thirty?
6. Do you pray throughout the day? If not, why not? If you do, how has it changed your life?
7. Are you going through a difficult time right now?
    a. Have you considered talking to a spiritual counselor, priest or pastor? Might it help to see a mental health counselor, psychologist, or physician?
    b. What gives you hope? Where do you see light?
    c. Do you surround yourself with people and things that help or harm your walk with God (including what you watch and read as well as other activities)?
    d. How can you become more intentional in guarding your eyes, ears, mind, and heart?
    e. How are you caring for your heart, mind, soul, spirit, and body during this time of difficulty or sorrow?

Before they call I will answer; while they are still speaking I will hear.
Isaiah 65:24

Your word is a lamp for my feet, a light on my path. I have taken an oath and confirmed it, that I will follow your righteous laws.
Psalm 119:105-106

We have this hope as an anchor for the soul, firm and secure.
Hebrews 6:19

Chapter 2 – Embraced by Love

1. Have you felt embraced by Christ's love?
   a. Recall the experience and consider writing it down.
   b. Have you ever shared this story with others? When was the last time? If you haven't, why not?
   c. Are you aware of Christ's love for you daily? Now? Brainstorm ways to become more aware of God's love every day.
   d. What spiritual disciplines can help you to live each day more aware of God's love for you?
2. If you haven't felt embraced by the love of God for a long time, would you pray now for God's love to fill you?
   a. Have you considered any obstacles (such as a need to forgive someone or let go of resentment) that may be keeping you from experiencing Christ's love more fully?
   b. Do you have a trusted spiritual counselor, mature Christian friend, a priest or pastor with whom you can pray?
3. Do you have a faith community that prays together, grows together, and keeps one another accountable? Do you participate actively?
4. Consider ways to use your gifts and talents to serve your church family and experience their love and gratitude as you love and care for them.

For I am convinced that neither death nor life, neither angels nor demons, neither the present nor the future, nor any powers, neither height nor depth, nor anything else in all creation, will be able to separate us from the love of God that is in Christ Jesus our Lord.
Romans 8:38-39

See what great love the Father has lavished on us, that we should be called children of God! And that is what we are!
1 John 3:1

You, God, are my fortress, my God on whom I can rely.
Psalm 59:17

Chapter 3 – The Importance of Yes

1. Have you spoken a final yes to God? How did it change your life?
2. If you haven't, what have you chosen instead (to what or to whom have you said yes)?
3. Would you like to say yes to God in a final way, or in a new and deeper way? I invite you to stop reading and pray now.
   a. What is stopping you now, if anything?
   b. Will it help to talk to a pastor, a priest, a mature Christian friend, or a trusted spiritual advisor?
4. What obstacles need to be removed so you can say yes to God and live according to His ways more intentionally? Why not do it now?
5. Are you aware of doors of grace that have opened wide as a result of your yes to God? Reflect on these gifts, thank God for them, and let them remind you of God's faithfulness whenever you go through tough times.
6. Consider journaling about answered prayers and/or times when you felt very close to God and refer back to your writing often.

For no matter how many promises God has made, they are 'Yes' in Christ.
2 Corinthians 1:20

*Yes, Lord, walking in the way of your laws, we wait for you; your name and renown
are the desire of our hearts.*
Isaiah 26:8

Yes, we will come to you, for you are the Lord our God.
Jeremiah 3:22

Chapter 4 – The Beginning of Relationship

1. Would you describe your experience of God as a relationship? If not, how would you describe it?
2. Do you want to recommit your life to God? Will you do it alone or with guidance from a trusted priest, pastor, or spiritual counselor?
3. How do you nurture your relationship with God?
   a. Do you read the Bible? Do you take time to meditate on God's Word and His purpose for your life?
   b. Do you pray throughout the day? Do you pray alone? Do you pray with other Christians?
   c. Do you worship in community consistently?
   d. Do you set aside time for silence, seeking to hear God's voice and to spend time with Him?
   e. Have you experienced the benefits of journaling as a spiritual discipline to help you discern God in your circumstances?
   f. Do you read books about faith or about people of faith?
   g. Have you discovered the power of praise?
   h. Do your answers reflect how much you value your relationship with God? If not, consider investing in one or two of these areas to deepen your walk with Christ.
4. What steps might you take to gain and nurture a more vibrant relationship with God?
5. How do you use your God-given gifts and talents to serve others?

But grow in the grace and knowledge of our Lord and Savior Jesus Christ.
2 Peter 3:18

Know that the Lord is God. It is he who made us, and we are his; we are his people, the sheep of his pasture.
Psalm 100:3

I pray that out of his glorious riches he may strengthen you with power through his Spirit in your inner being, so that Christ may dwell in your hearts through faith.
Ephesians 3:16-17

Chapter 5 – Healed by the Spirit

1. What instances of healing do you recall in your life? Consider spiritual, physical, and mental healing as well as healing of emotions and relationships.
2. What has been the relationship between your past or present healing and prayer?
3. Are you aware of God's active participation in your healing? Do you recognize this as an expression of God's love for you?
4. Do you ever think of God's healing as part of an ongoing relationship with God?
5. What is your role in healing? Do you hinder or help yourself heal and grow spiritually and emotionally?
6. Do the people in your life help you stay healthy and grow healthier?
7. What role does silence play in your ability to hear from God and receive healing and guidance?
8. Do you live with an attitude of gratitude toward the healing you've received and want to receive?
9. How does thanksgiving help keep you healthy and whole?

The Spirit of God has made me; the breath of the Almighty gives me life.
Job 33:4

The Spirit gives life; the flesh counts for nothing. The words I have spoken to you —
they are full of the Spirit and life.
John 6:63

Ask and it will be given to you; seek and you will find; knock and the door will be
opened to you.
Matthew 7:7

Chapter 6 – Why Yielding Means Freedom

1. What is hardest for you about surrendering to God's will?
2. As you reflect on your life, is it easier now to yield to God, or is it getting harder? Why?
3. Have you discovered freedom in saying a final yes to God? A daily yes to God?
4. What will make it easier for you to yield to God when you have a choice to make (e.g., when you need to forgive and don't want to, or when you need to give up your anger, resentment, or judgment)?
5. Do you feel free (spiritually, emotionally, mentally, and physically) or do you feel trapped or lost? Would it help to talk to a pastor, priest, or healthcare professional about the way you feel to gain greater freedom and control over your life?
6. Is there an area where you know you need to yield to God but you keep choosing not to yield?
    a. How is your choice helping you? Hurting you?
    b. Do you need help from someone else? Is it time to let go and trust God?

Let us not become weary in doing good, for at the proper time we will reap a harvest if we do not give up.
Galatians 6:9

Be kind and compassionate to one another, forgiving each other, just as in Christ God forgave you.
Ephesians 4:32

Follow God's example, therefore, as dearly loved children and walk in the way of love, just as Christ loved us and gave himself up for us as a fragrant offering and sacrifice to God.
Ephesians 5:1-2

Chapter 7 – A Thirst Quenched

1. Are you aware of an inner thirst and hunger for God? How do you nurture this longing for God and His ways?
2. Have you discovered music and praise as ways God feeds your soul and spirit?
3. Have you experienced God's Word as food for your soul?
   a. Are you growing in wisdom by applying God's precepts?
   b. Have you experienced greater peace as a result of meditating on God's Word and even memorizing it?
   c. Can you recall times when the Spirit brought to mind a Scripture you'd memorized exactly when you needed it?
4. Are there habits or addictions that harm your relationship with God and others? Have you sought help with these obstacles to your growth and abundant life?
5. Do you *worship* God at church, or is going to church more about meeting your needs?
6. Do you leave church and times of worship full of God's Spirit and emptied of self and anxiety? If needed, how might this change?
7. Do you ever ponder what it means to worship a holy God? How does this enhance your devotion to God and your worship?

My soul yearns for you in the night; in the morning my spirit longs for you.
Isaiah 26:9

Let anyone who is thirsty come to me and drink. Whoever believes in me, as Scripture has said, rivers of living water will flow from within them.
John 7:37-38

Do not get drunk on wine, which leads to debauchery. Instead, be filled with the Spirit.
Ephesians 5:18

Chapter 8 – Yearning for More

1. Do you want more success? Influence? A bigger platform? Material riches? A better job? A bigger house? A nicer car? Security?
   a. Where is God and His kingdom in your answers?
   b. Is God first, somewhere in the middle, or last? Be honest. This will help you know what to change, if anything.
2. Have you tasted God's living waters? Was it years ago, or is it an ongoing and frequent experience?
3. How do you nurture a hunger for God and His kingdom in your daily life?
4. Are your spiritual disciplines vibrant or stale?
   a. Is it time for a change?
   b. Can you commit to changing something starting now?
5. Have you discovered how reading books with sound teaching can increase your faith and keep you encouraged and on track?
6. Have you experienced that mentoring others on their faith journey helps you too?
7. Do you find that God is sufficient to meet all your needs? Why or why not?

I want to know Christ and the power of his resurrection and the fellowship of sharing in his sufferings.
Philippians 3:10

"Who is he who will devote himself to be close to me?" declares the Lord.
Jeremiah 30:21

They devoted themselves to the apostles' teaching and to fellowship, to the breaking of bread and to prayer.
Acts 2:42

Chapter 9 – God is Faithful

1. Have you experienced God and sensed His presence and activity in your life during the dark nights of your soul? How does recalling this help you during difficult times?
2. Have you experienced God's faithfulness? Recall specific times and consider sharing this with someone else.
3. How does God's faithfulness draw you to be more faithful to Him?
4. How would you explain the 3 Y's of faith to someone else?
5. Can you think of specific examples from your life of your experience with the 3 Y's?
6. Which Y is a greater challenge for you at this time, if any? Yes, Yield, or Yearn?
7. Do you feel at peace with God, or do you need to repent and/or return to Him?

And I pray that you, being rooted and established in love, may have power ... to grasp how wide and long and high and deep is the love of Christ.
Ephesians 3:17-18

Without faith it is impossible to please God, because anyone who comes to him must believe that he exists and that he rewards those who earnestly seek him.
Hebrews 11:6

Your love, Lord, reaches to the heavens, your faithfulness to the skies.
Psalm 36:5

Chapter 10 – Free to Love

1. Do you agree that the best way to exercise our God-given freedom is to love one another? Why or why not?
2. Is there someone you need to forgive? How will this help you live in greater freedom?
3. Are you aware of specific obstacles on your faith journey?
4. Do you see instances where pride, stubbornness, or self-sufficiency get in the way of what God wants to do in your life?
5. Are you ready to go deeper with God starting today?
6. What spiritual disciplines can you begin (or resume) starting now to help you prioritize and strengthen your relationship with God?
7. What may help you become more free to serve and love others with a light and cheerful heart?
8. Is there someone with whom you can discuss these questions and decisions to help keep you encouraged and accountable?

For this reason I remind you to fan into flame the gift of God, which is in you through the laying on of my hands. For the Spirit God gave us does not make us timid, but gives us power, love, and self-discipline.
2 Timothy 1:6-7

But seek first his kingdom and his righteousness, and all these things will be given to you as well.
Matthew 6:33

Therefore let us move beyond the elementary teachings about Christ and be taken forward to maturity.
Hebrews 6:1

About the Author

Amaryllis is married to a loving pilot-turned-preacher and is the happy mom of three terrific children. A prayer on her knees transformed her life years ago and turned her work as a family doctor into a ministry. She now sees herself as a servant in healthcare and strives to care for the soul and minister to the spirit while treating the body.

Through her writing and speaking ministry, Amaryllis responds to Mother Teresa's appeal to do "small things with great love." Her first book, *Walking with Jesus in Healthcare*, continues to inspire caregivers to stay close to God while caring for people. Based on the Gospel according to Luke (the physician), it encourages and equips healthcare professionals as well as their patients. Volume II awaits publication and will be based on The Acts of the Apostles (Dr. Luke's second book).

Amaryllis coauthored *The Ultimate Girls' Body Book*, an informative and fun book that helps girls navigate the challenges and embrace the joys of puberty. Written through Christian lenses, it inspires girls (and their moms) to see themselves as God's daughters and pursue God's best in every area of life.

A dynamic conference speaker and retreat leader, Amaryllis enjoys helping her peers in healthcare thrive despite a broken healthcare system in constant flux. Through coaching, she helps her colleagues identify and develop their gifts and rediscover ways to greater contentment, meaning, and purpose in medicine and in life.

Since 2001, Amaryllis has been blessed to write Bible commentary for *The Journey* and devotions for *Good News Daily* (www.biblereading.org). She enjoys helping people learn to feed their souls, renew their minds, and strengthen their spirits with God's Word and to apply its timeless principles in daily living.

Whether home with her family, working on a writing project, at a speaking engagement, or caring for people's medical needs, Amaryllis seeks to glorify God in all she does and to help others grow in their relationship with God.

She welcomes your comments, feedback, and requests to lead 3 Y's retreats at faithfulMD@gmail.com. For more information about her books and events, please visit her website.

Website: www.faithfulMD.wordpress.com

Blog: www.DrMarisFaithStop.com

Recommended Books for Spiritual Growth

Abide in Christ by Andrew Murray

Celebration of Discipline by Richard Foster

Hinds' Feet on High Places by Hannah Hurnard

Knowing Jesus Through the Old Testament by Christopher J. H. Wright

Mere Christianity by C. S. Lewis

My Utmost for His Highest by Oswald Chambers

Open Mind, Open Heart by Thomas Keating

Praying God's Word by Beth Moore

Ruthless Trust by Brennan Manning

The Battlefield of the Mind by Joyce Meyer

The Lamb's Supper by Scott Hahn

The Practice of the Presence of God by Brother Lawrence

The Return of the Prodigal Son by Henri Nouwen

The Screwtape Letters by C.S. Lewis

The Way of the Heart by Henri Nouwen

Other Books by the Author

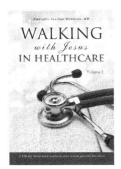

Walking with Jesus in Healthcare: A 120-day devotional to refresh your soul as you care for others

Join Dr. Mari and Dr. Luke as they walk with the Great Physician and learn how to care for people from the heart. No more ministering to people on your own strength. Abide in Jesus, the Healer, and you will minister out of his abundance and in the power of the Spirit. For more information, visit www.xulonpress.com/bookstore.

The Ultimate Girls' Body Book: Not-so-silly questions about your body

This fun and informative book helps girls and the adults who love them navigate the joys and challenges of puberty. Written by two family physicians through Christian lenses, it answers girls' top questions while helping them see themselves through God's eyes. For more information, visit www.zondervan.com.

To learn more about these and other resources, visit our website at
www.faithfulMD.wordpress.com

Journal

Journal

Journal

Journal

Journal

Journal

Journal

Made in the USA
Charleston, SC
16 August 2015